Kid's Get Learning

Educational books for kids

Money for Kids

Written by Tegan Helen

KIDS GET LEARNING

First published 2016 by 831 Designs Publishing
831designs.com

Why children need this book

Children really need to have and read this book lots, so they never have to get a job and work.

Losing your free time for fun things, to having to go work to get money instead.

If you learn everything in this book all about money and what to do with it, and really understand it all.

You will never need to work for money and your never to have a Job.

Money is everywhere and everything. If we can understand it and learn to control it, you will never have to work for money.

Let your money work for you so you can enjoy your life doing the things you enjoy doing.

If every kid only learns and does this one thing, we will all be rich no matter what we want to do when we grow up.

LET'S FIND OUT MORE.

For my parents,
David and Laura,

Who taught me that money does not make you happy,
but it helps.

If you can have your money work for you, then you can
enjoy life to the full.

For saving me and giving me the life that I deserve.
I love you both and owe you everything.

Support the NSPCC
10% of all author's royalties are donated to the

NSPCC
EVERY CHILDHOOD IS WORTH
FIGHTING FOR

Money for Kids

Hi I am Tegan Helen,

I have always loved writing and reading books.

What first made me want to be an author was reading Harry Potter and Robert Kiyosaki's, Rich Dad Poor Dad for Teens, in the book he said J.K. Rowling the author of Harry Potter had more money than the Queen.

Wow she gets to write fun stories that she loves to do, and people love to read them, so she makes lots of money and doesn't have to go to work, and helps people have fun.

It was not until my Muma saw an advert for UltraKids business event and Muma signed us up, then my book really took off, I kept thinking and dreaming I really want to be an author.

It was really hard thinking what children would enjoy and read every day, was a real challenge.

I love Roald Dahl, fairy books and Harry Potter books, these are good, but you do not learn anything?

Tegan Helen

I love to read my mums and Daddy's books as they are interesting, and I learn great things about how to get my dreams and be happy.

These do have a lot of tricky words in though, this made my bests idea, what to write about then I thought of "money for kid's"

I felt really proud of myself.

I really love writing books.

My little brother and I are both homeschooled, we are awesome kid's, because we are lucky and have awesome parents.

They are entrepreneurs and property investors who really help people, I have learnt a lot about money, they talk about it with us and explain where it comes from, where it goes, what it's all for, and what to do with it when we get it.

I can help other kids learn the great stuff like in my parents' books without having to get a dictionary for all the big words

Now I am seven and an author and a business owner.

Money for Kids

The clever way and the being a bit silly way.

I feel so lucky because when I am a grown up I will be able to choose if I want to work or have a job which I get paid for, or I can choose to do it the clever way keep on writing books and having a special and super fun life, instead of a boring job.

I think a lot of my friends who go to school and learn about stuff they don't like or must sit still and be quiet all day, don't have so much fun and when they finish big school they then must get a job, which only is enough to pay for the basics that they need. I feel this is a bit sad and really want to help a super load of kids.

If they learn the clever way and then they use the clever way, they can all have great fun lives too.

Don't Get Rich Quick, Get Rich For Sure!

Tegan Helen

Grant Cardone

Contents

How to Get Rich

Save a £1 every day for **compounding interest**

Work out your **income**

Write a **budget** and know what money you have

Make your **expenses** less

Stop buying **liabilities**

Save your money in a **high interest account**

Look for **income producing assets**

Work out your **profit**

Find a **good deal**

See if you can give a **deposit** for the good deal

Take out your saved money to buy **assets**

If you do not have enough money **borrow it.**

Know the difference of **good debt and bad debt**

If you borrow how much is the **interest.**

Can something be changed to make even more money.

Start back at the beginning

Keep doing this again and again.

If you start doing this when you are still only a kid, then when you get to be a grown up and live all by yourself instead of working hard in a job you will be able to choose to do what things it is that you love instead.

So, once you have enough assets getting you enough money (**passive income**) to pay for your expenses and the things you like and need in your life then you can buy liabilities, that is stuff you just really want for fun.

START NOW!

Compounding Interest

Compounding interest is the most exciting thing about money to learn about because anyone any age can do it, it takes time but is guaranteed to make you rich.

So, let me start by showing you how to do this with the example my parents first showed me.

If you put £1 a day away into a high interest account every day for 50 years you are guaranteed to be a millionaire!!!

And this is without adding in any extra money along the way, like Birthdays, Christmas, pocket money, jobs etc....

I find this super exciting because over time you put in very little money and get super loads out,

let me show you....

£1 a day after 1 year	= £385.53	you have put in £365
£1 a day after 10 years	= £6,997.70	you have put in £3650
£1 a day after 20 years	= £30,222.98	you have put in £7,300
£1 a day after 30 years	= £107,318.42	you have put in £10,950
£1 a day after 40 years	= £363,233.82	you have put in £14,600
£1 a day after 50 years	= £1,212,735.32	you have put in £18,250

WOW!! I know!!!

Because you get interest on top of interest on top of interest, this all really adds up over the years making you RICH!

You can see how little you put in **£18,250** and make over a MILLION POUNDS!!!!!

Now just dream if you put all the extra other money you get, in there too, this makes me crazy excited!

So, do you think you could find or make £1 every day?

If every kid only learns and does this one thing, we will all be rich no matter what we want to do when we grow up.

*Based on compounding interest at a rate of 12% per year (don't worry I will show you how to get 12% from your savings)

Income

Income is any money that you get for working, regularly pocket money, or paycheck from chores or a job.

It is up to you what you do with any money you get, some of it must be spent on expenses,

things you must buy.

The rest is up to you.

1. You can save it in a bank account or high interest savings account earning you extra money called interest.

2. You can use it to buy assets which you can make even more money and that will mean the money you get each month is even more.

3. Or you can use it to buy liabilities, things that you just want.

The choice is yours.

How to set up a Budget

Budgets are a great way to see how much money you have left to spend. They can be weekly or monthly budgets, It usually depends on when you get paid, either weekly or monthly.

First, you will need to write down any money that you get, this is called income. Which can be from pocket money, or odd jobs you have, or any profit from things you sell.

Add all these things together to give you the total of the income.

Then you need to write down, all your outgoing costs (expenses) that you buy each week or month, things like magazines, clothes, days out.

Then add all these things together to give you the total cost of your outgoings (expenses)

Then get your income total, take away your outgoings total and this will tell you how much money you will have leftover to spend or save. If your outgoings(expenses) are more than your income you will need to see where you can cut down your expenses or where you can make more money.

So, do you really need that magazine every time or new top or to spend so much on a day out?

Or you can sell more to make more or get a job do more chores.

You want to have money left over so that you can put it towards buying your assets which will give you more money and allow you to also give back.

Plan a Budget

Income:

Pocket money _____

Babysitting _____

Paper round _____

Cut lawns _____

Wash cars _____

Other _____

TOTAL INCOME: _____

Expenses

Make up _____

Hair gel _____

Phone credit _____

Clothes _____

Magazines _____

Days out _____

Other _____

TOTAL EXPENSES: _____

Total income _____ (minus) Total

Expenses _____

= _____ money left over.

Expenses

Expenses are things that you really need so you can live and be comfortable,

like shoes and clothes so that you can be warm and not hurt your feet.

Also, things like toothpaste, soap, food, water.

Somewhere to live and transport to get to places.

Your expenses should be much lower than any money that you are getting so that you can buy some assets, which will give you more and more each month.

If you have your expenses more than any money that you are getting you will have problems and struggle to pay for everything.

Also, you won't have any money left to buy assets which will give you more money.

Liabilities

Liabilities are things that takes money out of your pocket, things that you buy which costs you money.

The things that you just want are like the newest cool frozen toy or the new remote-control car, or the newest iPhone.

Once you spend the money on these cool new things all your money is gone from your pocket, you then must wait for more pocket money or for your next birthday or work like a paper round or something to get some more money.

If you only buy liabilities, you will need to keep working for more money and will always need a job.

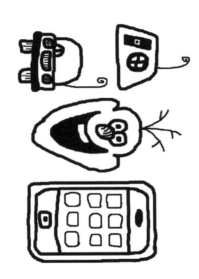

High Interest Account

Interest is money you pay (a fee that is paid) for borrowing money.

A fee is extra money that you pay as a thank you for the money.

If you have some money the interest works for you too.

If the bank borrows your money, then you get paid a fee to you each month.

If you are putting your money into a special savings account instead of a money box,

Then you really want the interest to be high, so you can get lots of extra money back each month,

instead of it just staying the same.

If you put £100 into the bank, you would get about £2 extra every year, this is called the interest.

Now it is about £2 each year because the bank pays 2% for borrowing the money from you.

This is about 17p each month.

But if you can find a good high interest account with a high % like 10-12%,

Like in **lendy.co.uk** then you can get £12 a year which is £1 a month, Wow that is a lot more huh!

And it is the same £100 you were going to put in your money box or in your bank account.

£200 will give you £2 a month

£300 will give you £3 a month

...it keeps getting better.

Assets

Something that puts money in your pocket, something you buy that gives you more money.

You buy something at a lower price and you sell it for more making you a profit.

Or you buy something that you can hire/lend it to people and they will give you money,

After they have finished you get your stuff back and get to keep the money you made as a profit. (extra money)

If you buy ten packets of crayons at 50p each and sell them at the village fete for £1 each,

Making a profit of 50p for each packet you sold,

So, **10 x 50p = £5.00**

You by some tennis rackets and some balls for £5

Then you let your friends borrow them for an hour to play tennis at the park for £1

At the end of the hour you get your tennis rackets back and keep the £1

After letting people borrow them five times you have the £5 back that it cost you so now every time you lend it out the money is all extra free money.

Remember that the rackets will get worn so save some of the extra money you make to by new ones later, so you can keep letting people borrow them.

Income Producing Assets

Income producing assets are something that puts money in your pocket every month for a long time. You buy something you can use, and you can get paid for using it.

You save your pocket money or get some for your birthday,

And instead of buying some new trainers for £60 you buy a lawnmower,

And offer to cut your neighbors garden for £5.

You do such a great job people tell their friends how good you are, and their friends want their gardens doing too

You now have four gardens to do every month,

If you want even more gardens you can make a poster and put them up somewhere or post them into people's houses that have gardens.

The great thing about grass is that it keeps on growing so they will need you again and again like every month, so it doesn't take long to get all the money back that you got for you birthday, then you can buy the trainers that you really wanted and still be making even more money next month.

If you buy an asset with the money you have and keep getting more money from those assets,

Then keep putting that money for even more assets then soon you will have enough money being given to you so then you can buy all the things you would like to have and still keep getting more money being given to you because you bought the assets first instead of just losing it all on one nice new thing.

Profit

Profit is when you sell something for more than you paid for it.

So, you buy a teddy for £5 and you sell it for £9 the extra £4 that you make is your profit. **(£9-£5=£4)**

To make sure you are working out the right profit, you need to make sure you take of all your fees you need to pay.

If you need to post the teddy and that costs you £1 you now have only got £3 profit **(£9-£5-£1=£3)**

Any other things you must pay for to sell it will be taken off too.

If you sell it on places like eBay or PayPal these also will charge you money for their help, this will also make your profit smaller.

Sell for		£9.00
Cost to buy	-	£5.00
Cost to post	-	£1.00
PayPal fees	-	£0.50
eBay fees	-	£0.90
TOTAL	**=**	**£1.60 PROFIT**

£1.60 profit does not sound like lots but if you sell 10 of them you will make £16 for no harder work.

So, you work one time and sell as many as you want to again and again.

Good Deal

What is a good deal?

How do you know if it is a good deal or not?

The bests deal you can get are the ones that...

1. Cost you only a little bit of money

2. Make you a big bit of money

3. Don't take too much time and work to do.

So, I am going to see what you think is the best deal out of three of my stories.

And why it is you think it is the best?

1. School tuck shop sells fruit at snack time for 50p for all the children to buy.

They have apples oranges and bananas.

I got out on the weekend and buy 2 punnets of strawberries.

They cost me £1.50 each.

I also bought a packet of 25 small plastic cups for 50p.

I put the strawberries into portions into the cups and sell them at snack time for 50p each.

I get 6 cups of strawberries out of each punnet.

Costs _____

Tegan Helen

Sold for _____

Extra money _____

(profit)

Was it hard work? _____

2) It is Halloween and we have a school disco, I told all my friends and all the people in my class that I am going to go to school early for the disco and paint everyone scary face paints for £1.

I bought a set of face paints crayon/pens for £2.50 Muma let me take two garden chairs to the disco.

I sat outside early, and my friends came to see me.

I painted 9 of my friends faces and they all paid me £1 each

And I painted my own face too.

Muma took the face paints and chairs home for me.

What's the sum?

What's the money I make?

Was it hard work?

Costs _____

Sold for _____

Extra money _____

(profit)

Was it hard work? _____

3) Me and my friends always play in the park when it is sunny and hot, we always hear the ice cream man with the music playing, sometimes our parents let us have one but lots of times they tell us no.

I went shopping with my family and asked my daddy if I could borrow £2 for a little while.

He said "yes", and I bought 2 boxes of choc ices, each box has 10 choc ices in it.

Next time we were playing in the park outside and the ice cream man came I said to all my friends I can get you all a choc ice same as mine for only 20p each, and I bet your mummy and daddy will always say yes to 20p.

That week I sold 19 choc ices and had one for myself. I paid my dad back and kept on getting more each week.

Was it hard work?

What's the money I make?

What's the sum?

Costs _____

Sold for _____

Extra money _____

(profit)

Was it hard work? _____

What money making idea made the most money?

1. _____

2) _____

3) _____

How could you make these even better/easier making more money?
To find out what I think and to share with me what your thoughts and ideas are.

Join me online at www.facebook.com/KidsGetLearning

Don't Just Make Money, Make a Difference!

Grant Cardone

Deposit

A deposit is when you want to buy something but do not have all the money you need to buy it.

You give the person/shop owner a smaller amount of money as a promise that you will buy the thing.

This also makes sure for you that they do not run out or sell the one you wanted, they will usually hold it back for you for a set time.

Then you go back each week/month and keep paying them money until the full price is paid,

and then you get to have it.

If you do not go back and make the other payments, you can lose the deposit because the person could have sold it to someone else when they were holding it back for you.

Then the person can sell it to someone else, so they can still make their money.

Borrowing money.

Debt is money that you borrow from someone,

You borrow money so that that you can buy something.

If it's not borrowed from Muma and Daddy, then you will have to pay interest each month.

You must keep paying interest until you have paid all the money back.

Bad debt

Bad debt is when you borrow some money and pay back the interest which is costing you money each month for liabilities, things that you don't really need, but just want, new frozen toys, new remote-control car of the new iPhone.

Good debt

Good debt is when you borrow some money to buy an asset, this then means you will be able to pay back the interest and money you borrowed each month, with the money from the asset.

Buying an income producing asset, which pays you more money than the money you must pay back is great debt!

Interest

Interest is extra money you pay when you borrow money as a thank you for the borrowing service.

If you borrow some money you must pay it all back and pay a bit extra, this is what they call interest.

If you are borrowing money like a loan, then you really want the lowest smallest interest you can, so you only must pay back a little extra.

But if you can only get a higher one, if the income producing assets still makes you more money, then that's ok too.

Passive income

Imagine you're not at work,

you do not want to go to work,

but you can still make money without working all week.

Your money works for you.

Sounds like magic doesn't it?

You work one time and keep on getting paid and getting paid without having to work again and again.

That is what I want to do,

I really get excited about this one,

This is why I wrote this book for children.

If I spend a long week writing this book and doing my bestest,

If people love it and keep buying it then I have made my first passive income.

Because I only need to write it one time then it gets printed into loads of books then I can sell loads of books again and again and again, but I only had to write it one time.

It's all about having enough income producing assets which pays you money each month which covers all your expenses and enough for you to enjoy life.

Giving Back

There is a saying...

"Money is the root of all evil"

Which means money is bad.

Money is not bad, if it is used in a good way.

I love to give back which is why every book that I sell 10% goes to the NSPCC which is a charity close to my heart.

Also, when I go shopping with my Muma I buy something to go into the trolley for the homeless people, things like cereal or biscuits, some yummy stuff that they can smile when they eat it.

With assets you buy and the money that you get, what are you going to spend it on?

Who are you going to get to help you?

The more money you can make, the more people you can help!

When you can help people, it makes me feel so happy that I can make someone else smile or make a kid be safe.

NSPCC - my chosen charity

I support the NSPCC as this is a charity that is very important for children Just like me.

It is like a nightmare that is not nice.

This is why I am supporting this charity.

I was with mean parents, now I am safe with good parents,

Now I am happy and that is why I love to help this charity,

So, it helps the children that need it.

Why I wanted to be an Author.

1. To become Famous!

2. So, people can learn and have fun lives.

3. So, people do not need to go to work.

4. To help children with the NSPCC

5. And to make a passive income

How I became an Author in only 20 days

1. Sign up to a business event for kid's

2. Really understand and focus on my why I want to do this?

3. Write first draft with what I have already learnt.

4. Daddy read through my draft and teaches me other great stuff.

5. I asked lots of questions and learned cool stuff to put in the book.

6. I write up the second try and design a logo.

7. My Muma makes my logo look awesome and designs my business cards and banner.

8. When I finish my second try, I get Daddy to read it again, he helps me change a few things, and makes sure I really understand this great stuff.

9. I draw the pictures that I think other kids will like.

10. I write my actual book no mistakes and lots of cool stuff to learn.

11. I help my Muma type up the book and draw pictures.

12. I write all about me, so you can see why I am doing this.

13. We sent the book off to the printers

14. I wrote a few blogs

15. I start practicing vlogging

16. Book comes back and is totally awesome so exciting!!!

17. Muma helps me set up a website and a Facebook and LinkedIn accounts.

18. I practice talking about my book and answering questions which is really easy.

19. I get an early night, I am super excited!!

20. Kid's business show hopefully sell my books!!

Notes.

Notes.

How I Met Grant Cardone

I first met Mr. Grant Cardone in his office in Miami, Florida, we dropped by in the hope of seeing him and we had a meeting in his office with him and his wife Elena Cardone.

He has a lot of things with his logo on and he has even got his own baseball bat and fish tank, it looked awesome.

I asked him lots of questions and we talked for a while before Grant Cardone and I went to his studio where he does his daily Facebook shows.

I asked him "If you could not leave your daughters money, what would you leave them."

He responded, "The idea that they can do anything." Wow what a powerful belief to give your children. His second answer was "that they need to help a lot of people, as the more people they help, the more friends they have and the more friends they have, the better they will do in life." I loved his answers, what a great parent and example he is for his girls.

He learnt to become who he is today. With the resources that he had, buying something for $1 selling it for more, keep buying more to sell more. Consistency is key

I gifted him one of my books for his two girls and he gave me a great sales quote book, a chocolate airplane of his private jet and The Millionaire Handbook, this is the second-best book that you will read, and I recommend you read this next, this Money for Kids book is the FIRST.

He was super exited to give my book to his girls, sharing with me his recent discussions he has had with his girls, about assets and investments, creating passive incomes. I am excited for his feedback.

I then asked if I could have 15 minutes on his stage to share my story to inspire his audience, if an 8-year-old can write a book and hustle, then any one can. He said, "I cannot promise that, but if you show up, it becomes more possible and we can make magic happen". I did show up, I attended his 10x Growth conference in Las Vegas. He had so many speakers and a few on them over ran their time so instead he gave me an opportunity to sell my books. I was so excited, I hustled hard and I sold 150 books in 2 days and made over $3000.

On the last day I went backstage and thanked and hugged Grant Cardone. For giving me the opportunity to watch the amazing speakers and to sell my Money for Kids book.

I loved meeting Grant Cardone he was really cool. I was really fortunate to meet many incredible people out there making a positive impact in this world.

I recommend going to 10x Growth Conference. You can check out where and when at 10xGrowthCon.com also do not forget to buy The Millionaire Handbook.

KIDS GET LEARNING

If you loved reading this as much as I loved writing this then please connect with me.

I would love to hear your thoughts.

http://kidsgetlearning.com

https://www.facebook.com/KidsGetLearning

To keep updated and to find out when the next book will be release, sign up to my newsletter.

newsletter@kidsgetlearning.com

My Dad for helping me write this book and spending time to teach me this cool, useful stuff.

My Muma for editing and illustrating the images throughout the book.

For Janet Young for the photo of me on the front cover.

facebook.com/janetyoungwadebridge

For alerrandre for producing the front and back covers

flickr.com/photos/alerrandre01

I dedicate this book to my little brother Tyler David for giving me, the motivation and I look forward to teaching

him over the coming years.

831

Made in the USA
Columbia, SC
05 June 2021